TOP 10 OLYMPIC CHAMPIONS

BY JOHN WALTERS

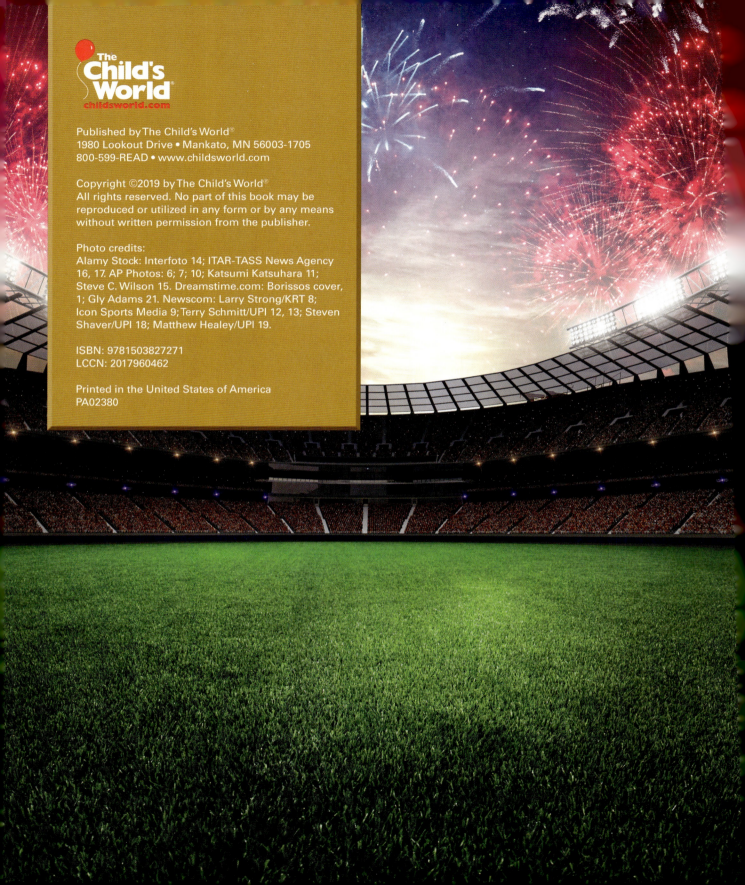

Published by The Child's World®
1980 Lookout Drive • Mankato, MN 56003-1705
800-599-READ • www.childsworld.com

Photo credits:
Alamy Stock: Interfoto 14; ITAR-TASS News Agency
16, 17. AP Photos: 6; 7; 10; Katsumi Katsuhara 11;
Steve C. Wilson 15. Dreamstime.com: Borissos cover,
1; Gly Adams 21. Newscom: Larry Strong/KRT 8;
Icon Sports Media 9; Terry Schmitt/UPI 12, 13; Steven
Shaver/UPI 18; Matthew Healey/UPI 19.

ISBN: 9781503827271
LCCN: 2017960462

Printed in the United States of America
PA02380

CONTENTS

WHO'S NUMBER ONE?

The problem with ranking Olympic athletes is that they are all so different! More than 400 gold medals are awarded in each Summer and Winter Olympics. Athletes compete on ice, in water, or on snow. They ride bicycles, horses, and sailboats. They throw a javelin, a discus, or a shot put. They even throw themselves off a ski jump!

Olympians come in every shape and size that humans come in. You've got tall basketball players. There are tiny gymnasts and skaters. There are enormous weightlifters.

Usain Bolt

NUMBERS, NUMBERS

American Ray Ewry was great at something sort of odd. He could jump very far and high . . . without a run-up. He won eight gold medals from 1900 to 1908. His events? Standing high, long, and triple jumps. His best standing long jump was 11.3 feet. See how far you can jump that way!

In the winter, big, strong athletes push bobsleds, while athletes of all sorts take part in the low-key sport of curling. And athletes who have overcome physical challenges take part in the Paralympics.

How do you compare their skills? Sprinters run fast. Divers spin and plunge. Snowboarders flip and fly. Some athletes took part in many Olympics, while others shined only in one.

Choosing who is the all-time best is an Olympian job!

That's where you come in. We've narrowed the list down to our Top 10. These are some of the most successful Olympians ever. Most of them competed before you were born. You might have to read even more to make your choices. But read on and make your own Top 10. Who knows? Maybe some day you will be find yourself on this list, too!

Larisa Latynina

NADIA COMANECI

GYMNASTICS
ROMANIA

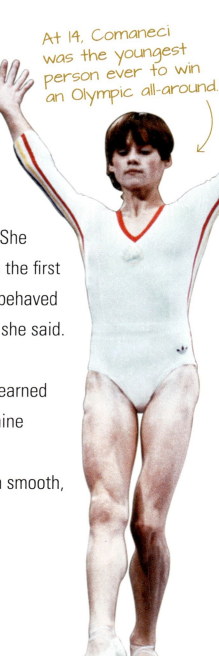

At 14, Comaneci was the youngest person ever to win an Olympic all-around.

For a long time, a perfect 10 was the best possible score in gymnastics. Until 1976, no one had ever gotten one. At the 1976 Olympics in Montreal, someone did. Romania's Nadia Comaneci was the first to get a 10. She was only 14!

Her first event was the **uneven parallel bars**. She flipped, flew, and landed. The score went up. It was the first perfect 10 ever! The fans went wild! The tiny teen behaved as if it were no big deal. "I knew it was **flawless**," she said. "I have done it 15 times before."

Comaneci won three gold medals in 1976. She earned two more golds in Moscow in 1980. In all, she got nine perfect scores in Olympic events.

Through it all, she amazed judges and fans with smooth, artistic skills. She was pure perfection.

NUMBERS, NUMBERS
Comaneci was the first person to score a perfect 10 at the Olympics. She also ended up with more such scores than any other gymnast, male or female.

6

SONJA HENIE

FIGURE SKATING
NORWAY

Sonja Henie made this list for being the only person to win three gold medals in figure skating. She also deserves a spot for her impact on the sport. Her skill, elegant style, and clothing changed her sport.

Henie was born in Norway. She was a top tennis player when young. She switched to skating, and became a champion. In 1924, she skated in her first Olympics. She came in last place! Well, she was only 11 years old!

Four years later, Henie was the Olympic champion. Fans and judges loved her smooth, flowing style. She made skating beautiful. She repeated as Olympic champ in 1928 and 1932.

Henie also won a record 10 world championships.

Henie was the first Winter Olympic athlete to become world famous. She skated in popular ice shows in Europe and the United States. She also became a popular movie actress. Not surprisingly, she skated in all her movies! She was one of the first female sports superstars.

NUMBERS, NUMBERS

Following her Olympic career, Sonja acted in 15 Hollywood films. The most famous were *Sun Valley Serenade* and *Thin Ice*.

7

JACKIE JOYNER-KERSEE

Jackie Joyner-Kersee was the best female athlete in the history of Olympic track and field. Other women have won more gold medals, thanks to **relay** events. But "JJK's" three individual golds are the most ever.

The 1988 Seoul Olympics were her biggest moment. She entered the Games under lots of pressure. *Sports Illustrated* had called her "Superwoman." Joyner-Kersee was up to the challenge. She won the **heptathlon** with a record score. That seven-part event calls for strength and speed. Women run, jump, and throw, all in two days.

Five days later, she won gold again. She set an Olympic record in the long jump.

Gold ran in Joyner-Kersee's family. Her brother Al won the 1984 Olympic triple jump. Her sister-in-law, Florence Griffith-Joyner, won three sprinting golds in 1988.

Four years later, she was under more pressure to repeat. Once again, she came through. She won her third gold medal. She remains the only two-time Olympic champion in the difficult heptathlon.

NUMBERS, NUMBERS

In 1988, Joyner-Kersee set a world record in the heptathlon. Her score of 7,291 points remains the best ever, more than 30 years later.

CARL LEWIS

TRACK & FIELD
UNITED STATES

In 1991, Lewis ran the 100 meters in 9.86 seconds. That was the fastest time ever to that point.

No one thought Jesse Owens could be matched. In 1936, that great runner won four gold medals at the Berlin Olympics. In 1984, however, American star Carl Lewis won the 100- and 200-meter sprints. He captured the long jump gold. He got his fourth win in the sprint relay.

Owens could not add to his total. World War II canceled two Olympic Games. Lewis took part in four Olympics. In those Games, he won five more gold medals. He became the first person to win the long jump four times. He got another relay gold. And in 1988, he was the 100-meter champion again.

Only two other Olympians have matched Lewis's record of winning four gold medals in the same event. Al Oerter did it in the discus throw. Swimmer Michael Phelps won a **quartet** of 200-meter individual **medleys**. Meanwhile, Lewis is the best American track and field athlete of all time.

NUMBERS, NUMBERS

Between 1981 and 1991, Lewis won 65 long jump meets in a row. That's still an all-time record!

PAAVO NURMI

They called him the "Flying Finn." But he didn't fly . . . he ran! Between 1920 and 1928, Finland's Paavo Nurmi was virtually unbeatable on the track. He ran distances of 800 meters or more. He was the most **dominant** Summer Olympics athlete until Michael Phelps came along.

Nurmi entered 12 Olympic races. He ran from 1500 meters to 10,000 meters. He won nine of them! In the other three, he finished second and earned silver medals. Over the course of his brilliant career, he set 22 world records. At the 1924 Olympics, Nurmi won five golds. He won the tough 1,500-meter and 5,000-meter races in the same afternoon.

The oldest of five children, Nurmi lost his father when he was 11. His family crowded into a single-room apartment. He never allowed poverty to stop him from doing his best.

Nurmi is the only runner to hold world records in the mile, 5,000- and 10,000-meter races at the same time.

NUMBERS, NUMBERS

At the peak of his career, Nurmi won 121 races in a row. He won at distances of 800 meters and longer.

10

TRISCHA ZORN

SWIMMING
UNITED STATES

Trischa Zorn has won more gold medals than any swimmer in history. She has not seen any of them, however. Zorn is the most successful Paralympic athlete ever. She won 41 gold medals and 55 total medals from 1980 to 2004. Zorn swims in the Games that are held for athletes who face physical challenges. Zorn is blind.

The Paralympics started in 1960. They are open to athletes who have lost arms or legs, or who are blind or paralyzed in some way. The athletes compete against people with similar disabilities. Zorn began swimming when she was 10. By the time she was 16, she was a champion. She is a legend in the Paralympic community. The U.S. Swimming Federation even named an award after her!

← Zorn swam several strokes, including freestyle, backstroke, and butterfly.

NUMBERS, NUMBERS
From 1980 to 1992, Zorn won an amazing 25 Paralympics races in a row.

USAIN BOLT

TRACK & FIELD
JAMAICA

This star from Jamaica is the greatest sprinter in Olympic history. Much like his races, it isn't even close. Usain Bolt was the first person to win both the 100-meter and 200-meter sprints in three Olympics in a row. He won from 2008 to 2016. He won in Beijing, London, and Rio de Janeiro. That's not all! In all three Games, he also ran the **anchor leg** of gold-medal-winning 4x100-meter relay teams. (Later, he had to give back his 2008 relay gold. One of his teammates was caught using illegal drugs.)

NUMBERS, NUMBERS

The three fastest 100-meter times in history belong to Bolt.

Year	Time
2009	9.58
2012	9.63*
2008	9.69

*Olympic record

At 6-5, Bolt is the tallest person ever to set the 100-meter world record. Bolt's height allows him to run the race in 41 strides. Most other runners need 43 to 45.

At 6 feet and 5 inches, Bolt stood out because he was so tall. Most sprinters are at least five inches shorter. Even under pressure, Bolt seemed at ease. Before races, he always appeared relaxed. After each win, he broke out his famous pose. He pointed one arm into the sky and formed a "bolt" with his other arm!

Unlike most top sprinters, he was slow at the start. He used his long legs to catch up, though. By the end of many races, he was far ahead. Sometimes, he could look back and smile at his opponents! He used that speed to break world records in the 100 and 200 meters. He also won 11 World Championships medals.

It will probably be a long time before anyone beats Bolt's records. Until then, he's the "Fastest Man in the World."

ERIC HEIDEN

SPEEDSKATING
UNITED STATES

The Winter Olympics have been held since 1924. Thousands of athletes have skied, skated, and snowboarded. None, however, have come close to matching what Eric Heiden did in 1980. The American speedskater won five gold medals at the Lake Placid Games. That's the most by an athlete in a single Winter Games. What was more amazing was that he won such different races. Imagine a track runner winning the 100 meters . . . and the 5,000 meters!

Heiden entered events at five distances: 500, 1,000, 1,5000, 5,000, and 10,000 meters. The Wisconsin **native** won all five races, and he set Olympic records in four of them.

His final race, the 10,000, is more than 6 miles.

In 1980, Heiden won more golds than most countries! Only two nations topped him. The Soviet Union won 10. East Germany won nine.

Heiden set one of his records and beat his opponent by more than 100 yards.

Heiden had a couple of things going for him. He worked hard to build massive thighs. They were more than 29 inches around! He used those legs to power his skating. His other advantage was his attitude. He did not act like a big star or show off after he won. He was very humble, but still determined to win. Even as he was becoming a world hero, he still went to other events. He cheered for his American teammates all over Lake Placid! Now, every Winter Olympian has Heiden's great feats to aim for.

NUMBERS, NUMBERS
They Came Close

Here are two Olympians who came closest to Heiden, with four golds in one Winter Olympics.

Athlete, Nation	Sport	Year
Lydia Skoblikova, USSR	Speedskating	1964
O.E. Bjorndalen, Norway	Biathlon	2002

LARISA LATYNINA

GYMNASTICS
SOVIET UNION

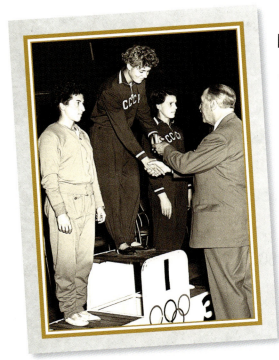

Larisa Latynina is the queen of Olympic athletes. No female athlete has ever won more than her nine gold medals. None have topped her 18 overall medals, either. In fact, only one male Olympian has surpassed her: Michael Phelps (page 18).

Latynina did not have an easy childhood. She was born in the communist Soviet Union in 1934. Her father left the family before her first birthday. He was later killed in a World War II battle in Stalingrad. The Soviets were fighting invaders from Nazi Germany. Her mother could not read. She had to work two jobs, including one as a security guard. She was not around to help Latynina very much. World War II ended in 1945. That's when Latynina took up ballet at age 11.

NUMBERS, NUMBERS

Here's the full list of Laytnina's medals:

1956
Gold: team, all-around, vault, floor exercises
Silver: uneven bars
Bronze: team apparatus

1960
Gold: team, all-around, floor exercises
Silver: uneven bars, balance beam
Bronze: vault

1964
Gold: team, floor exercises
Silver: all-around, vault
Bronze: uneven bars, balance beam

After she stopped competing, Latynina became a coach. She led the Soviet Union's women's teams to gold medals in 1968, 1972, and 1976.

The dance studio closed a year later. So she switched to gymnastics. She turned out to be a natural. She competed in the 1956, 1960, and 1964 Olympics. All three times, she led her nation to the team gold medal. All three times, she earned the gold in the floor exercises. She combined her skills at ballet with powerful leaps and tumbling. Latynina also earned gold in the 1956 and 1960 all-around and the 1956 **vault**. Along the way, she picked up several silver and bronze medals.

In 2016, Phelps at last broke her record for most Olympic medals. Latynina was in the stands in London cheering him on. "Phelps deserves the record, he is such a talented sportsman," Latynina said graciously.

Of course, she added, "Among women, I'm sure I will stay number one for a long time."

She's right. The next closest female to Latynina is Marit Bjørgen of Norway. That cross-country skiing star has 14 total medals. Latynina's record is safe.

MICHAEL PHELPS

It's one thing to have pressure put on you. Most top athletes know what that feels like. In the case of Michael Phelps, he put the pressure on himself. No athlete in Olympic history ever faced a bigger challenge than Phelps did in 2008. He had already won six Olympic golds at the 2004 Athens Games. For 2008 in Beijing, he signed up to compete in *eight* races. Michael Phelps was clear in wanting to beat American swimmer Mark Spitz's record of seven golds in one Olympic Games.

Phelps said, "I want to be the first Michael Phelps, not the second Mark Spitz."

Phelps first discovered the swimming pool in third grade. He was

battling ADHD. He had trouble sitting still in class. It was hard to concentrate. His mom thought swimming would help. It did that . . . and more! Phelps took to the water like a fish.

Phelps has appeared in five Olympics. That's more than any male U.S. swimmer in Olympic history. "If you dream as big as you can dream," he once said, "anything is possible."

Seven years and lots of hard work later, he went to his first Olympics in 2000. He was just 15 years old! He got his first medals at the 2004 Games. That set up his record run in China.

Under great pressure, he did it! Phelps won all eight events to set a new single-Olympics record. He was not finished. He kept winning for two more Olympics, 2012 and 2016. When he finally climbed from the pool for good, he had earned a stunning total of 23 golds! Add in silvers and bronzes and his total was 28 medals! Both those marks are far more than any other Olympian, male or female, Summer or Winter.

NUMBERS, NUMBERS

Eight is considered a lucky number in China. The opening ceremony for the Beijing Olympics took place on August 8, 2008. That can be written 8-8-08. Phelps won a record eight gold medals at those Beijing Games. Phelps probably thinks it's pretty lucky, too!

YOUR TOP TEN!

In this book, we listed our Top 10 Olympians. We gave you some facts and information about each athlete. Now it's your turn to put the players in order. Find a pen and paper. Now make your own list! Who is the No. 1 Olympic champion of all time? How about your other nine choices? Would they be the same athletes as we chose? Would they be in the same order? Are any athletes missing from this book? Who would you include? Put them in order—it's your call!

Remember, there are no wrong answers. Every fan might have different choices in a different order. Every fan should be able to back up their choices, though. If you need more information, go online and learn. Or find other books about these great athletes. Then discuss the choices with your friends!

THINK ABOUT THIS . . .

Here are some things to think about when making your own Top 10 list:

• What sport did he or she play?

• Did they take part in multiple Olympics?

• How long have their records lasted?

• What impact did they have on their sport or on the Games?

SPORTS GLOSSARY

anchor leg (ANK-er LEG) the final segment of a relay race

butterfly (BUT-ur-fly) in swimming, a stroke in which the arms are both flung forward at the same time

dominant (DAHM-ih-nent) overpowering, unbeatable

flawless (FLAW-less) perfect

heptathlon (hep-TATH-lon) a women's track event that includes seven events of running, jumping, and throwing

medleys (MED-leez) in swimming, races in which more than one type of stroke is used

native (NAY-tiv) born in a particular place in the world

quartet (kwor-TET) a group of four

relay (REE-lay) in track and swimming, a race in which a series of athletes each cover part of the entire distance

uneven parallel bars (un-EE-ven PAYR-uh-lel BARZ) a women's gymnastics event that uses two raised bars, one higher than the other

vault (VAWLT) a gymnastics event in which athletes leap over a low barrier and do moves before landing

FIND OUT MORE

IN THE LIBRARY

Gray, Karlin. *Nadia: The Girl Who Couldn't Sit Still.* New York, NY: HMH Books for Young Readers, 2016.

Markovics, Joyce. *Michael Phelps: Amazing Americans.* New York, NY: Bearport Publishing, 2017.

Mason, Paul. S*ports Heroes of Ancient Greece.* New York, NY: Crabtree, 2010.

ON THE WEB

Visit our Web site for links about Top 10 Olympic athletes: **childsworld.com/links**

Note to Parents, Teachers, and Librarians: We routinely verify our Web links to make sure they are safe and active sites. So encourage your readers to check them out!

INDEX

ABOUT THE AUTHOR

John Walters wrote for *Sports Illustrated* and *Newsweek* and worked for NBC Sports at the Summer Olympics. He earned two Sports Emmys for his work there. He is the author of *The Same River Twice: A Season With Geno Auriemma and the Connecticut Huskies*, *Notre Dame Golden Moments*, and a coauthor of *Basketball for Dummies*.